KES

A play of the novel

by

BARRY HINES
and
ALLAN STRONACH

HEINEMANN EDUCATIONAL BOOKS
LONDON

Heinemann Educational Books Ltd

LONDON EDINBURGH MELBOURNE AUCKLAND TORONTO
SINGAPORE HONG KONG KUALA LUMPUR
IBADAN NAIROBI JOHANNESBURG NEW DELHI
LUSAKA KINGSTON

ISBN 0 435 23500 1

All rights whatsoever in this play are
strictly reserved. Any enquiries concerning amateur
and professional performing rights should be made
before rehearsal to: Sheila Lemon, Spokesmen,
1 Craven Hill, London W2 3EP. No
performance may be given unless a licence has been
obtained.

Published by
Heinemann Educational Books Ltd
48 Charles Street, London W1X 8AH
Filmset in 10/11 Garamond by
Spectrum Typesetting Ltd, London,
and printed in Great Britain by
Biddles of Guildford, Martyr Road,
Guildford, Surrey

Contents

Introduction

Kes, the play, grew from the need of a group of school students to find a contemporary play they could not just perform but also associate themselves with. Having read the novel they were already able to sympathize with many of the situations and characters in the story of *Kes*.

The resulting play is intentionally episodic presenting in 23 scenes aspects of the life of fifteen-year-old Billy Casper during his final months at school. Initially it is the story of a boy obtaining and training a kestrel hawk but it is also about much more as well. It is not the training of the hawk that is the important thing in the relationship between boy and bird but rather the attitude that Billy has towards Kes that makes him able to train it. More than anything it is an attitude of respect, admiration and affection.

Attitude is also the theme with which other aspects of the play are concerned. As well as his attitude to Kes it is also about Billy Casper's attitudes towards the people he knows and meets and about their attitudes towards him.

We see the Casper household and attitudes between Billy, Mrs Casper and step-brother Jud on four occasions. Billy's only real attempt at conversation with his family, when he begins to tell his mother of his plan to get a kestrel and build a hut for it, is quickly rebuked when she realizes she is late for her evening out.

During the scenes when Billy is at school we are able to see the attitudes of both his superiors and his peers. Only on three short occasions is he given any real consideration by anyone who represents the school system. Mr Farthing, the English teacher, twice attempts a conversation with Billy personally and is partially successful each time. The third, and most successful occasion that the school has anything to offer is when—once again encouraged by Farthing—Billy is able to hold the full attention of the class as he relates, through his experiences, how he first 'obtained' and then trained Kes.

Apart from these three occasions the school not only has nothing to offer Billy but through its refusal to admit as much repeatedly rebukes him from all sides. His classmates spend much time poking fun at him because he has strayed from the norm and prefers the company of Kes to that of his peer group.

The Headmaster, even with a full 30 years' teaching experience behind him, administers the cane rather than find out the reason why Billy fell asleep during morning Assembly. Sugden, the P.E. teacher, using the double weapon of sarcasm and authority gives Billy a miserable time during the Games lesson. Even the Youth Employment Officer becomes easily exasperated with the realization that not only has the school been unable to offer Billy anything but neither can he.

Billy Casper stands, of course, as a representative of a significant proportion of our school populace today. He is even more representative because at the end of it all he merely resigns himself to the facts. Billy Casper, however, has the advantage over the majority in that he has been able to experience something that neither home nor school could offer him. In having known and trained Kes he has had something to both admire and respect.

Cast of First Production

The original production of *Kes* was presented at Colley School, Sheffield in April 1974 with the following cast:

Bill Colton	Philip Rogers
Paul Allender	Gary Palmer
Kim Beatson	Karen Bream
Steven Hawley	Alan Jackson
Michael Tyson	Philip Baker
Ian Aldridge	Jayne Salisbury
Albert Nelson	John Bellamy
Rosemary Barr	Nigel Holmes
Diane Stephenson	Douglas Gilberthorpe
Stephanie Wilson	Alison Manning
Frank Brightmore	Linda Goodwin
David Burns	Jasmine Peacock
Steven Cartledge	Vicki Mackley
Michael Holmes	Maureen Brown
Shaun Allen	Fiona Worthington
Alex Morton	David Spillings
Paul Timmins	Trevor Bradshaw
Steven Martin	Darrell Hepworth
Andrew Camm	Tina Hattersley
Terry Connolly	Sylvia Spillings
Kevin Fox	Christine Thompson
Adrian Onerearnshaw	Jayne Saxton
John Delamore	Cheryl Woodruff
Glyn Gibbs	

KES

List of Characters

ACT ONE

Scene 1: BILLY AND JUD'S BEDROOM AND KITCHEN

BILLY *and* JUD *are asleep in the same bed. Quiet. The alarm clock rings.* BILLY *fumbles for it, eventually finds it and switches it off.*

BILLY: Bloody thing. (*Pause*)
  Jud! (*Pause*)
JUD: What?
BILLY: You'd better get up. (*Pause*) Alarm's gone off you know.
  know.
JUD: Think I don't know? (*Pause*)
BILLY: Jud.
JUD: What?
BILLY: You'll be late.
JUD: Oh, shut it.
BILLY: Clock's gone off you know.
JUD: I said 'shut it!' (*He thumps Billy.*)
BILLY: Gi'oer, that hurts.
JUD: Well shut it then.
BILLY: I'll tell mi' mam about you.
  JUD *slowly gets out of bed. He finally finds his trousers and puts them on.*
BILLY: Set alarm for me Jud. For seven.

3

JUD: It's nearly that now.

BILLY: It's not

JUD: It's late. Clock's wrong.

He pulls the bedclothes off Billy.

BILLY: You rotten sod.

JUD: Get up then.

JUD goes into the kitchen for breakfast. He finds himself some bread and jam on the table. BILLY *slowly gets dressed and joins him. He looks at the clock in the kitchen.*

BILLY: Have you seen the time?

JUD: 7 o'clock gone.

BILLY: You're late.

JUD: Hour and half.

JUD pours himself a cup of tea. He drains the pot which means there is none for Billy.

BILLY: Smashing morning again.

JUD: You wouldn't be saying that if you were going where I'm going.

BILLY: Just think, when I'm doing 'papers you'll be going down in the cage.

JUD: Yeh. And just think, in a few weeks you'll be coming down wi'me.

BILLY: I'll not.

JUD: Won't you?

BILLY: No, because I'm not going to work down the pit.

JUD: Where you going to work then?

BILLY *has a drink of milk from the bottle.*

BILLY: I don't know, but I'm not going to work down the pit.

JUD: No, and shall I tell you why? (*He puts his jacket on.*) For one thing, you've to be able to read and write before they'll let you down the pit. And for another, they wouldn't have a weedy little bugger like you.

JUD goes out. He has left his 'snap' on the table. BILLY *eventually sees it, opens it and begins to eat one of the sandwiches. He is halfway through it when* JUD *returns.*

JUD: I've forgot my snap. (BILLY *finishes off the sandwich, gets up and hurries off to his paper round.*) I'll murder you when I get home. And don't bother with your bike—I've already got it.

MR PORTER *is carefully arranging newspapers on the counter when* BILLY *enters.*

MR PORTER: I thought you weren't coming.

BILLY: Why, I'm not late am I? (PORTER *looks at his pocket watch.*) I nearly was though.

MR PORTER: What do you mean?

BILLY: Late. Our Jud went to the pit on my bike.

MR PORTER: What you going to do then?

BILLY: Walk it.

MR PORTER: And how long do you think that's going to take you?

BILLY: Not long.

MR PORTER: Some folks like to read their papers the day they come out, you know.

BILLY: It'll not take me that much longer. I've done it before.

MR PORTER: 'Cos there's a waiting list a mile long, you know, for your job. Grand lads as well some of them, from up Firs Hill and round there.

BILLY: What's up. I haven't let you down have I?
A MAN *on his way to work enters the shop.* MR PORTER'S *attitude changes immediately.*

MR PORTER: Morning Sir. Nice again.

MAN: Twenty Players please.

MR PORTER: Certainly Sir. Thank you.
THE MAN *pays and goes out.*

MR PORTER: You know what they said when I took you on don't you? They said—'you'll have to keep your eyes open now, you know, 'cos they're all alike off that estate. They'll take your breath if you're not careful.'

BILLY: I've never taken anything of yours, have I?

MR PORTER: Never had chance, that's why.

BILLY: I've stopped getting into trouble now.

MR PORTER: Come on then, you'll be wanting me to take them round for you next. (*He climbs a ladder to begin stacking things on the shelves.*)

5

BILLY: What time is it?

MR PORTER: A quarter to eight.

BILLY: Already? (*He squeezes past the ladder to get his pile of newspapers from behind the counter.*)

MR PORTER: You'll be late for school. Mind you, I wouldn't like to think it was my job trying to learn you 'owt.

BILLY *squeezes past the ladder again and shakes it on purpose.*

BILLY: Look out, Mr Porter. You're all right, I've got you.

MR PORTER: You clumsy young bugger. What you trying to do. Kill me?

BILLY: I lost my balance.

MR PORTER: I wouldn't put it past you either. (*Descends ladder and feels his heart.*) I fair felt my heart go then.

BILLY: Are you all right now, Mr Porter?

MR PORTER: All right? Aye, bloody champion.

BILLY: I'll be off then.

MR PORTER: And don't be late for tonight's.

Scene 3: BILLY MEETS THE MILKMAN

THE MILKMAN *is about to deliver two pints of milk to a house.*

MILKMAN: How's it going then, young 'un.

BILLY *stops and leans.*

BILLY: Oh, not so bad.

MILKMAN: You could do wi' some transport. That milk float's better than walking you know.

BILLY: Ay, only just, though. They only go five miles an hour them things.

MILKMAN: Still better than walking though.

BILLY: I could go faster on a kid's scooter.

MILKMAN: You know what I always say?

BILLY: What?

MILKMAN: Third class riding's better than first class walking any day.

BILLY: I'm not so sure with one of them things.

MILKMAN: Please yourself. See yer.

BILLY: See yer.

Scene 4: BILLY'S HOUSE

BILLY *enters the house and puts his paper-round bag away.*

MRS CASPER: Oh, it's you Billy. Haven't you gone to school yet?

BILLY: 'Brought my bag back.

　　MRS CASPER *picks up an empty cigarette packet.*

MRS CASPER: You've not got a fag on you have you? (*He doesn't reply.*) There's tea mashed if you want a cup. I don't know if there's any milk left.

　　BILLY *goes to pour himself a cup of tea, but there is none left.*

MRS CASPER: Do me a favour love, and run to the shop for some cigarettes.

BILLY: They'll not be open yet.

MRS CASPER: You can go to the back door. Mr Hardy'll not mind.

BILLY: I can't. I'll be late.

MRS CASPER: Go on love, bring a few things back with you.

BILLY: Go yourself.

MRS CASPER: I've no time. Just tell him to put it in the book and I'll pay him at the weekend.

BILLY: He says you can't have anything until you've paid up.

MRS CASPER: He always says that. I'll give you 5p when you come back.

BILLY: Don't want 5p. I'm off.

MRS CASPER: Come here, will you?

BILLY: I'm not mam, I'll be late for school.

MRS CASPER: Just you wait 'till tonight. An' there's a bet of our Jud's to take an 'all. Don't forget that.

BILLY: I'm not taking it.
MRS CASPER: You'd better lad.
BILLY: I'm fed up of taking 'em. He can take it himself.
MRS CASPER: How can he when he's not back home in time.
BILLY: I don't care, I'm not taking it. I'm off.
MRS CASPER: You just wait. You'll see.

Scene 5: MAC'S HOUSE

BILLY *throws pebbles up to the window of MacDowall's house.*

BILLY: Mac. Mac.

   MRS MACDOWALL *comes to the window and leans out.*
She pulls her dressing gown tight as it is cold.
BILLY: Is he up?
MRS M.: What do you want at this time?
BILLY: Is your Mac up?
MRS M.: Course he's not up, this time on a Saturday.
BILLY: Isn't he getting up?
MRS M.: Not that I know of. He's fast asleep.
BILLY: He's a right 'un. We're going bird nesting. It was his idea.
MRS M.: Stop shouting will you?
BILLY: He's not coming then?
MRS M.: No, he's not. You'd better come back after dinner if you want to see him. (*She closes the window.* BILLY *throws a handful of dirt at it and* MRS MACDOWALL *reappears.*) Bugger off you little sod.

   BILLY *goes bird nesting by himself.*

Scene 6: WATCHING A KESTREL

BILLY *is sitting watching a kestrel that has been collecting food for its young, which are nesting in an old monastery wall. The farmer, who the field belongs to, appears.*

FARMER: Hey. What are you doing?

BILLY: Nothing.

FARMER: Go on then. Don't you know this is private property?

BILLY: No! Can I get up to that kestrel's nest?

FARMER: What kestrel's nest?

BILLY: Up that wall.

FARMER: There's no nest up there, son.

BILLY: There is. I've just been watching it fly in. (*Pause*)

FARMER: And what you going to do when you get up to it. Take all the eggs?

BILLY: There's no eggs in, they're young 'uns.

FARMER: Then there's nothing to get up for then is there?

BILLY: I just wanted to look, that's all.

FARMER: And you'd be looking from six feet under if you tried to climb up there.

BILLY: Can I just have a look from the bottom then? I've never found a hawk's nest before. That's where it is, look, in that hole in the side of that window.

FARMER: I know it is, it's nested here donkey's years now.

BILLY: Just think, and I never knew.

FARMER: There's not many that does.

BILLY: I've been watching them from across in the wood. You ought to have seen them. One of them was sat on that telegraph pole for ages. I was right underneath it, then I saw its mate. It came from miles away and started to hover just over there. Then it dived down behind that wall and came up with something in its claws. You ought to have seen it mister.

FARMER: I see it every day. It always sits on that pole.

BILLY: I wish I could see it every day. Has anybody ever been up that wall to look.

FARMER: Not that I know of. It's dangerous. They've been going to pull it down for ages.

BILLY: I bet I could get up.

FARMER: You're not going to have the chance though.

9

BILLY: If I lived here I'd get a young 'un and train it.
FARMER: Would you? (*Pause*)
BILLY: You can train them.
FARMER: And how would you go about it? (*Pause*)
BILLY: Do you know?
FARMER: No, and there's not many that does. That's why I won't let anyone near, because if they can't be kept properly it's criminal.
BILLY: Do you know anyone who's kept one?
FARMER: One or two. Not many.
BILLY: Where could you find out about them?
FARMER: Books I suppose. I should think there are books on falconry.
BILLY: Think there'll be any in the library?
FARMER: Could be in the City library. They've books on everything there.
BILLY: I'm off now then. So long mister. (*Runs off.*)
FARMER: Hey!
BILLY: What?
FARMER: Go through that gate. Not over the wall.

Scene 7: THE PUBLIC LIBRARY

THE LIBRARIAN *is sitting at her desk. Others are looking at the bookshelves.* BILLY *enters.*

BILLY: Got any books on hawks missis?
LIBRARIAN: Hawks?
BILLY: I want a book on falconry.
LIBRARIAN: I'm not sure. You'd better try under ornithology.
BILLY: What's that?
LIBRARIAN: Under Zoology.
  BILLY *goes to look for the shelf.*

10

LIBRARIAN: Hey!

BILLY: What?

LIBRARIAN: Are you a member?

BILLY: What do you mean, a member?

LIBRARIAN: A member of the library.

BILLY: I don't know owt about that. I just want a book on falconry. That's all.

LIBRARIAN: You can't borrow books unless you're a member.

BILLY: I only want one.

LIBRARIAN: Have you filled one of these forms in? (BILLY *shakes head.*) Well, you're not a member then. Do you live in the borough?

BILLY: What do you mean?

LIBRARIAN: The Borough, the City!

BILLY: No, I live on the Valley estate.

LIBRARIAN: Well that's in the Borough isn't it?

A customer has a book stamped out. BILLY *just stands looking round in the library.*

BILLY: Can I get a book now then?

LIBRARIAN: You'll have to take one of these forms home first for your father to sign.

BILLY: My Dad's away.

LIBRARIAN: You'll have to wait till he comes home then.

BILLY: I don't mean away like that. I mean he's left home.

LIBRARIAN: Oh, I see . . . well in that case your mother'll have to sign it.

BILLY: She's at work.

LIBRARIAN: She can sign it when she comes home, can't she?

BILLY: She'll not be home till tea time and it's Sunday tomorrow. I want a book today.

LIBRARIAN: Then you'll just have to wait, won't you?

BILLY: Just let me go an' see 'f you've got one, an' if you have I'll sit down at one o' them tables and read it.

LIBRARIAN: You can't. You're not a member.

BILLY: Nobody'll know.

LIBRARIAN: It's against the rules.

BILLY: Go on. I'll bring you this paper back on Monday then.

Another customer hands a book to the Librarian to be stamped out. They chat pleasantly about the weather. BILLY *sees the zoology shelf and goes to it. He quickly finds a book*

about hawks, puts it under his jacket and quickly goes out of the library, past the two still talking at the desk.
BILLY: Ta-ra.

Scene 8: BILLY'S HOUSE

BILLY *is quietly sitting reading the book from the library when* JUD *enters.*

JUD (*getting ready to go out for the night*): What do you want that for, when you can't read? (*Snatches the book from him.*)
BILLY: Give it me back. Come here.
JUD: Falconry? What do you know about falconry?
BILLY: Give it me back.
JUD: *A Falconer's Handbook.* Where have you got this from?
BILLY: I've lent it.
JUD: Nicked it more like. Where have you got it from?
BILLY: The library in town.
JUD: You must be cracked.
BILLY: How do you mean?
JUD: Nicking books. I could understand it if it was money but chuff me, not a book.
BILLY: I've been reading it all afternoon. I'm nearly halfway through.
JUD: And what better off will you be when you've read it?
BILLY: A lot because I'm going to get a young kestrel and train it.
JUD: You couldn't train a flea. Anyroad, where you goin' to get a kestrel from?
BILLY: I know a nest.
JUD: You don't.
BILLY: All right then I don't.
JUD: Where is it?
BILLY: I'm not telling.

JUD: I said where? (*Pushes* BILLY'S *face into cushion and puts his arm up his back.*) Where?

BILLY: Give over Jud, you're breaking my arm.

JUD: Where, then?

BILLY: Monastery farm. (JUD *lets go.*)

JUD: I'll have to see about going round there with my gun.

BILLY: I'll tell the farmer if you do, he protects them.

JUD: Protects them. Don't talk wet. Hawks are a menace to farmers, they eat all their poultry and everything.

BILLY: I know, they dive down on their cows and carry them away an' all.

JUD: Funny bugger.

BILLY: Well, you talk daft. How big do you think they are? kestrels only eat insects and mice and little birds sometimes.

JUD: You think you know something about them don't you?

BILLY: I know more about them than you anyroad.

JUD: You ought to an' all. You nearly live round in them woods. It's a wonder you don't turn into a wild man. (JUD *scratches his armpits and runs round the room imitating a wildman.*) Billy Casper, wild man of the woods. I ought to have you in a cage, I'd make a bloody fortune.

BILLY: I was laid watching them for hours this afternoon.

JUD: I'm hoping I'll be laid watching a bird tonight, but she won't have feathers on.

BILLY: You ought to have seen them though Jud.

JUD *is tying his tie.*

JUD: A few pints first.

BILLY: You ought to have seen them dive down.

JUD: Then straight across to the club.

MRS CASPER *enters.*

MRS CASPER: You're a couple of noisy buggers. What you tormenting him for Jud?

JUD: I never touched him.

BILLY: Not much. He nearly broke my arm, that's all.

JUD: I'll break your neck next time.

MRS CASPER: O shut it both of you.

JUD: Well he's nothing but a big baby.

BILLY: And you're nothing but a big bully.

MRS CASPER: I said shut it. (*Pause*)
Where you going tonight then?

JUD: Usual I suppose.

MRS CASPER: And don't be coming home drunk again. Seen my shoes Billy love?

JUD (*looking into the mirror*): Some bird's going to be lucky tonight. (*He goes out.*)

MRS CASPER (*picking her shoes up*): They could have done with a polish. Still, never mind, it'll soon be dark. There's no ladders in these stockings is there Billy?

BILLY (*without looking*): Can't see any.

MRS CASPER: What you going to do with yourself tonight love?

BILLY: Read my book.

MRS CASPER: That's nice. What's it about?

BILLY: Falconry. I'm going to get a young kestrel and train it.

MRS CASPER: That's nice. I say, what time is it?

BILLY: I've cleaned the bottom shed out ready, an' I've built a little nesting box out of an orange box, 'til . . .

MRS CASPER: Ten to eight. I'm going to be late as usual. Here, there's 10p for you. Go and buy yourself some pop and crisps or something. Ta-ra.

BILLY *reads aloud but hesitantly. It is important to hear him struggling with the language.*

BILLY: The kestrel is about 12-14 inches long. The male is slightly larger than the female and both sexes have reddish-chestnut plumage with black spots on their upper parts and buff plumage with brownish streaks below. In level flight the kestrel has a silhouette typical of the falcons: a large head, broad shoulders, long pointed wings and quite a long tail. It can hover in the air for minutes on end when hunting. When it is doing so its tail is fanned and its head is inclined downwards. It lives in many different types of places: mountains and hills, open moors, farmland, suburbs and even city centres on occasions.

Lights fade.

Scene 9: JUD RETURNS HOME

BILLY *is now in bed reading the book to himself when he hears Jud come into the house. He switches off the bedside lamp and pretends to be asleep.* JUD *enters. He is drunk.*

JUD: Billy. Billy. (*He is swaying gently.*) Are you ashleep Billy?
(*He begins to get undressed, humming a pop tune he has been hearing all night while still gently swaying. He tries to take off his trousers but begins to lose balance.*)
Whoa you bugger, whoa. Billy wake up. Billy. (*Pulls at bedclothes.*) Wake up Billy I said.

BILLY: Give over Jud, I'm asleep.

JUD: Help me get undressh Billy. I'm drunk. I'm too drunk to get undreshed. (*He drops onto the bed giggling.*) Help me Billy.
BILLY gets out of bed and takes JUD'S *trousers off for him.*

BILLY: I'm fed up of this game. It's every Saturday night alike. (JUD *snores loudly.*) Just like a pig snoring—a drunken pig. Jud the drunken pig. He stinks. You stink. Jud the stinking, drunken pig. (*He shuts* JUD'S *mouth.*)

JUD: What's a matter? What's a matter?

BILLY: Go back to sleep you pig—hog—sow—drunken bastard. (*He starts tapping* JUD.) Pig—hog—sow—drun—ken—bas—tard. (*He repeats this and as the chant gets louder, so the slaps get harder.*)

BILLY: Pig—hog—sow—drun—ken—bas—tard.
Pig—hog—sow—drun—ken—bas—tard.
He eventually thumps JUD *who makes a loud noise and tries to sit up.* BILLY *grabs his own trousers and runs out of the bedroom.*

Scene 10; MORNING ASSEMBLY

The classes come into the School Hall noisily, accompanied by various members of staff. When MR GRYCE *comes onto the platform they immediately go quiet.*

GRYCE: Hymn No. 175— 'New Every Morning is the Love'
(*They begin turning pages, coughing, making a fuss, etc.*)
Stop that infernal coughing! It's every morning alike. As soon as the hymn is announced you're off.
(*Pause. Then a lone voice coughs.*)
Who did that? I said who did that. (*No one owns up.*) Mr Crossley. Somewhere near you. Didn't you see the boy?
(CROSSLEY *pushes his way into the lines.*) There Crossley! That's where it came from! Around there!
(CROSSLEY *grabs hold of* MACDOWALL.)
MACDOWALL: It wasn't me sir.
CROSSLEY: Of course it was you.
MACDOWALL: It wasn't sir, honest.
CROSSLEY: Don't argue lad, I saw you.
GRYCE: Macdowall. I might have known it was you. Get to my room lad.
(MACDOWALL *leaves the hall.*)
Right. We'll try again. Hymn 175. (*They sing the first verse very poorly.*)
GRYCE: Stop! And what is that noise supposed to represent? I've heard sweeter sounds in a slaughter house! This is supposed to be a hymn of joy—not a dirge. If that's the best you can do, we won't bother. The whole school will therefore return to this hall after school is over. Then you'll sing. Or I'll MAKE you sing like you've never sung before. We'll now say the Lord's Prayer. Heads Bowed. Our Father . . .

(The school join in the Lord's Prayer. After it is finished GRYCE *tells them to sit down.* BILLY *who is day-dreaming about being with Kes does not hear him and so remains standing.)*

GRYCE: Casper. Casper. (BILLY *opens his eyes and sits down.*) Up Casper. Up on your feet lad. Silence! *(Pause)* You were asleep, weren't you?

BILLY: I don't know sir.

GRYCE: Well I know. You were fast asleep weren't you? Fast asleep during the Lord's prayer. Were you tired lad?

BILLY: I don't know sir.

GRYCE: Don't know? You wouldn't be tired if you got to bed at night instead of sitting up till dawn watching some tripe on television. Report to my room now. You will be tired when I've finished with you. (BILLY *goes.*)

NOTICES: There will be a meeting of the intermediate football team in the gym at break this morning. A reminder that the Youth Employment Officer will be in this afternoon to see the Easter leavers. You all know the time of your appointments. Be there. Finally I would like to see the three members of the smoker's union whom I didn't have time to deal with yesterday. They can pay their dues at my room after assembly. Right, dismiss.

Scene 11: HEADMASTER'S STUDY

THE THREE SMOKERS, BILLY *and* MACDOWALL *are waiting for the Headmaster to return.*

MACDOWALL: It wasn't me that coughed you know. I'm going to tell Gryce that an' all.

1ST SMOKER: It makes no difference whether you tell him or not, he doesn't listen.

MACDOWALL: I'll bring my father up if he gives me the stick anyway.

BILLY: What you always bringing your father up for? He never does anything when he comes. They say last time he came up, Gryce gave him stick as well.

17

MACDOWALL: At least I've got a proper father to bring up, that's more than you can say Casper.

BILLY: Shut your gob, Macdowall.

MACDOWALL: Why, what you going to do about it?

BILLY: You'd be surprised.

MACDOWALL: Right then, I'll see you at break.

BILLY: Anytime you want.

MACDOWALL: Right then.

BILLY: Right.

Pause. A SMALL BOY *enters with a message for Gryce.*

1ST SMOKER: If you've come for the stick you'd better get to the back of the queue.

MESSENGER: I've not come for the stick; Crossley's sent me with a message.

Pause.

MACDOWALL: It's his favourite trick this. He likes to keep you waiting. He thinks it makes it worse.

2ND SMOKER (*takes cigarettes etc. out of his pocket and goes to the boy*): Here, you'd better save us these until after. If he searches us he'll only take them off us and give us another two strokes.

MESSENGER: I don't want them, you're not getting me into trouble as well.

2ND SMOKER: Who's getting you into trouble. You can give them back after.

MESSENGER (*shaking head*): Don't want them.

2ND SMOKER: Do you want some fist instead?

THE THREE SMOKERS *surround him and fill his pockets with cigarettes, lighters etc.*

BILLY: Hey! He's here. Gryce Pudding.

GRYCE *enters.* BOYS *stand in a line.*

GRYCE: Right you reprobates. (*They go in.*) The same old faces. Why is it always the same old faces?

MESSENGER: Please sir.

GRYCE: Don't interrupt boy, when I'm speaking. (*He walks down the line.*) I'm sick of you boys, you'll be the death of me. Not a day goes by without me having to see a line of boys. I can't remember a day—not one day—in all the years that I've been in this school, and how long's that? . . . ten years, and the school is no better now than it was on the day it opened. I can't understand it, I really can't. (*He goes to the window and admires the neatly cut lawns outside. He remains there as he continues talking.*) I thought I understood young people. I should be able to with all my experience—I've taught in this city thirty-five years now—but there's something happening today that's frightening. It makes me feel that it's all been a waste of time. (THE BOYS *look at each other, bored.*) Like it's a waste of time talking to you boys now, because you're not taking a blind bit of notice of what I'm saying. I know what you're thinking now, you're thinking why doesn't he shut up and get on with it. That's what you're thinking isn't it? Isn't it Macdowall?

MACDOWALL: No sir.

GRYCE: Of course it is. I can see it in your eyes lad, they're glazed over.

MESSENGER: Please sir.

GRYCE: Shut up lad. As far as I can see there's been no advance at all in discipline, decency, manners or morals. And do you know how I know this? Because I still have to use this every day. (*He takes the cane from the top of his desk.*) I can understand why we had to use it back in the twenties and thirties. Those were hard times, they bred hard people and it needed hard measures to deal with them. We knew where we stood in those days; they bred people with respect for a start. Even today a man will stop me in the street and say—'Hello Mr Gryce, remember me?' And we'll pass away the time of day and he'll laugh about the thrashings I used to give him. (THE BOYS *have stopped listening altogether by now.*) They took it then, but not now. Not in this day of the common man, when every boy quotes his rights and shoots off home for his father as soon as I look at him . . . No guts . . . no backbone . . . you've nothing to commend you whatsoever. (*He swishes the stick in front of them.*) So for want of a better solution I continue using the cane, knowing full well that you'll be back time and time again for some more. You smokers will carry on smoking just the same. (*One of the smokers is smirking at the other boys.*) Yes you can smirk lad. I bet your pockets are ladened up in readiness for break this very moment, aren't they? Aren't they? Well just empty them, come on, get your pockets emptied.

THE THREE SMOKERS, BILLY *and* MACDOWALL *begin to empty their pockets.*

MESSENGER: Please sir . . .

GRYCE: Quiet lad and get your pockets emptied. (*He moves along the line inspecting the contents distastefully.*) This can't be true, I don't believe it. (*He puts the stick back on the desk.*) Keep you hands out. (*He goes along the line again frisking their clothing. He finally comes to the young boy.*) Ah! Ah!

MESSENGER: Please sir . . .

GRYCE: You're a regular little cigarette factory aren't you? (*He methodically takes the objects from the boy's pockets.*) You deceitful boy. You didn't think you could get away with a weak trick like that, did you? (*He puts all the objects into the basket.*) Right, one at a time, over here.

THE THREE SMOKERS, BILLY, MACDOWALL *and the* BOY *individually come to the headmaster's desk, lean over it and are given two strokes each. It is important that this is done as realistically as possible and it should certainly not be funny in any way at all.* THE THREE SMOKERS, BILLY *and* MACDOWALL, *although it hurts them, take it in their stride. As Gryce has already suggested, they will probably be back for more on another occasion. When it is the* MESSENGER'S *turn, however,* GRYCE *has to direct him to the table and he leaves the room crying.*

Scene 12: THE ENGLISH LESSON

MR FARTHING *is giving books out to the class when* BILLY *walks in.*

BILLY: I've just been to see Mr Gryce, sir.

MR FARTHING: Yes, I know. How many this time?

BILLY: Two.

MR FARTHING: Sting?

BILLY: Not bad.

MR FARTHING: Right, sit down then. (*Pause as* BILLY *sits down.*) Right . . . Anderson. We've been talking about fact and fiction. I want you to stand up and tell us something about yourself—a fact—that is really interesting.

ANDERSON: I don't know anything sir.

MR FARTHING: Anything at all Anderson. Something that's happened to you, which sticks in your mind.

ANDERSON *begins to smile.*

ANDERSON: There's something but it's daft though.

MR FARTHING: Well, tell us then and let's all have a laugh.

ANDERSON: Well it was once when I was a kid. I was at junior school, I think, or somewhere like that, and went down to Fowlers Pond, me and this other kid. Reggie Clay they called him, he didn't come to this school; he flitted and went away somewhere. Anyway it was Spring, tadpole time, and it's swarming with tadpoles down there in Spring. Edges of the pond are all black with them, and me and this other kid started to catch them. It was easy, all you did, you just put your hands together and scooped a handful of water up and you'd got a handful of tadpoles. Anyway we were mucking about with them, picking them up and chucking them back and things, and we were on about taking some home, but we'd no jam jars. So this kid, Reggie, says, 'Take your Wellingtons off and put some in there, they'll be all right 'til you get home.' So I took them off and we put some water in them and then we started to put taddies in them. We kept ladling them in and I said to this kid, 'Let's have a competition, you have one Wellington and I'll have the other, and we'll see who can get most in!' So he started to fill one Wellington and I started to fill the other. We must have been at it hours, and they got thicker and thicker, until at the end there was no water left in them, they were just jam packed with tadpoles. You ought to have seen them, all black and shiny, right up to the top. When we'd finished we kept dipping our fingers into them and whipping them up at each other, all shouting and excited like. Then this kid said to me, 'I bet you daren't put one on'. And I said, 'I bet you daren't.' So we said we'd put one on each. We wouldn't though, we kept reckoning to, then running away, so we tossed up and him who lost had to do it first. And I lost, oh, and you'd to take your socks off as well. So I took my socks off, and I kept looking at this Wellington full of tadpoles,

21

and this kid kept saying, 'Go on then, you're frightened, you're frightened'. I was as well. Anyway I shut my eyes and started to put my foot in. OOoo, it was just like putting your feet into live jelly. They were frozen. And when my foot went down, they all came over the top of my Wellington and when I got my foot to the bottom, I could feel them all squashing about between my toes. Anyway, I'd done it, and I says to this kid, 'You put yours on now'. But he wouldn't, he was dead scared, so I put it on instead. I'd got used to it then, it was all right after a bit; it sent your legs all excited and tingling like. When I'd got them both on I started to walk up to this kid, waving my arms and making spook noises; and as I walked they all came squelching over the tops again and ran down the sides. This kid looked frightened to death, he kept looking down at my Wellingtons so I tried to run at him and they all spurted up my legs. You ought to have seen him. He just screamed out and ran home roaring. It was funny feeling though when he'd gone; all quiet, with nobody there, and up to the knees in tadpoles.

MR FARTHING: Very good Anderson. Thank you. Now has anyone else got anything interesting to tell us all. (*No hands go up.* BILLY *is fidgeting on his chair after receiving the cane.*) What about you Casper? (BILLY *does not hear him.*) Casper!

BILLY: What sir?

MR FARTHING: Have you been listening?

BILLY: Yes sir.

MR FARTHING: Then tell us what we've been talking about.

BILLY: Er . . . stories sir.

MR FARTHING: What kind of stories?

BILLY: Er . . .

MR FARTHING: You don't know, do you?

TIBBUT: He's been asleep again sir.

BILLY: Shut your gob Tibbut.

MR FARTHING: Casper. Tibbut. You'll both be asleep in a minute. I'll knock you to sleep. (*Class are quiet.*) Right Casper you can do the work for a change. You're going to tell us a story—just like Anderson—any story at all, about yourself. Stand up.

BILLY: I don't know any sir.

MR FARTHING: I'm giving you two minutes to think of something lad, and if you haven't started then the whole class is coming back at four.

(*Immediate reaction from the class. Various pupils shout out.*)

HOLMES: Come on Billy.

CARTLEDGE: Or else you die!

BAKER: Say anything.

BARR: If I've to come back I'll kill him.

MR FARTHING: I'm waiting Casper. (*Pause*)

BAKER: Tell him about your hawk Casper.

MR FARTHING: If anyone else calls out it will be the last call he'll make . . . What hawk Casper? . . . Is it a stuffed one? (*The whole class laugh.* BILLY *is upset and he wipes his eyes.*) What's so funny about that? Well Tibbut?

TIBBUT: He's got a hawk sir, it's a kestrel. He's mad about it. He never comes out with anybody else now, he just looks after this hawk. He's crackers with it.

BILLY: It's better than you anyday Tibbut.

MR FARTHING *sits down. Pause.*

MR FARTHING: Now then Billy, come on, tell me about this hawk . . . where did you get it from?

BILLY *is looking down at his desk.*

BILLY: Found it.

MR FARTHING: Where?

BILLY: In a wood.

MR FARTHING: What had happened to it; was it injured?

BILLY: It was a young one. It must have tumbled from a nest.

MR FARTHING: And where do you keep it?

BILLY: In our shed.

MR FARTHING: Isn't that cruel?

BILLY *looks at him for the first time.*

BILLY: I don't keep it in the shed all the time. I fly it every day.

MR FARTHING: And doesn't it fly away? I thought hawks were wild.

BILLY: 'Course it doesn't fly away. I've trained it.

MR FARTHING: Was it difficult.

BILLY: 'Course it was. You've to be right . . . right patient with them and take your time.

MR FARTHIN: Come out here then and tell us all about it.

(BILLY *goes out hesitatingly*.) Right, how did you set about training it?

BILLY: I started training Kes when I'd had him about a fortnight. He was as fat as a pig though at first. You can't do much with them until you've got their weight down. Gradually you cut their food down, until you go in one time and they're keen. I could tell with Kes because he jumped straight on my glove as I held it towards him. So while he was feeding I got hold of his jesses.

MR FARTHING: His what?

BILLY: Jesses. He wears them on his legs all the time so you can get hold of them as he sits on your glove.

MR FARTHING: And how do you spell that?

BILLY: J—E—S—S—E—S.

MR FARTHING: Right, tell us more.

BILLY: Then when he's on your glove you get the swivel —like a swivel on a dog lead, then you thread your leash—that's a leather thong—through your swivel, do you see?

MR FARTHING: Yes, I see. Carry on.

BILLY: So you wrap your leash round your fingers so Kes is now fastened to your hand. When you've reached this stage and he's feeding from your hand regular and not bating too much . . .

MR FARTHING: Bating . . . what's that?

BILLY: Trying to fly off, in a panic like. So now you can try feeding him outside and getting him used to things. (BILLY *is now becoming more confident in telling his story*.) But you start inside first, making him jump onto your glove for the meat. Every time he comes you give him a scrap of meat. A reward like. Then when he'll come about a leash length straight away you can try him outside, off a fence or something. You put him down, hold onto the end of the leash with your right hand and hold your glove out for him to fly to. (BILLY *is now doing the basic mime actions to accompany the story*.) When he's done this a bit you attach a creance instead of a leash—that's a long line, I used a fishing line. Then you put the hawk down on the fence post. Then you walk into the middle of the field unwinding the creance and the hawk's waiting for you to stop and hold your glove up. It's so it can't fly away you see.

MR FARTHING: It sounds very skilful and complicated Billy.

BILLY: It doesn't sound half as bad as it is though. I've told you in a couple of minutes but it takes weeks to do all that. They're as stubborn as mules, hawks. Sometimes he'd be all right, then next time I'd go in the shed and he'd go mad, screaming and bating as though he'd never seen me before. You'd think that you'd learnt him something, you'd put him away feeling champion and then the next time you went you were back where you started.

MR FARTHING: You make it sound very exciting though.

BILLY: It is, but the MOST exciting thing was when I flew him free for the first time. You ought to have been there then. I was frightened to death.

MR FARTHING (*turning to the class*): Do you want to hear about it?

CLASS: Yes sir.

MR FARTHING: Carry on Casper.

BILLY: Well, I'd been flying him on the creance for about a week and he was coming to me anything up to thirty, forty yards. It says in the book that when it's coming this far, straight away, it's ready to fly loose, I daren't though I kept saying to myself, I'll just use the creance today to make sure, then I'll fly it free tomorrow. I did this for about four days and I got right mad with myself. So on the last day I didn't feed him up, just to make sure that he'd be sharp set the next morning. I hardly went to sleep that night, I was thinking about it that much. When I got up next morning—it was a Saturday—I thought right, if he flies off, he flies off and it can't be helped. So I went down to the shed. He was dead keen as well, walking about on his shelf behind the bars and screaming out when he saw me coming. So I took him out on the field and tried him on the creance first time and he came like a rocket. So I thought right, this time. I unclipped the creance and let him hop onto the fence post. There was nothing stopping him now. He could have flown off and there was nothing I could have done about it. I was terrified. I thought, he's forced to go, he's forced to go. He'll just fly off and that will be it. But he didn't. He just sat there looking round while I backed off into the field. I went right into the middle. Then I held my glove up and shouted him. (*He is miming the action.*) Come on Kes, come on then. Nothing happened at first. Then just as I was going to walk back to him, he came. Straight as a die, about a yard off the floor. He came twice as fast as when he had the creance on. He came like lightning, head dead still and his wings never made a sound. Then wham! Straight onto the glove, claws out grabbing for the meat. I was that pleased I didn't know what to do with myself, so I thought, just to prove it, I'll try him again, and he came the second time just as good. Well that was it. I'd trained him. I'd done it.

MR FARTHING: Right, that was very good. I enjoyed that and I'm sure the class did as well.

Splatter of applause from the class, BILLY *sits down.*

Scene 13: BREAKTIME

BILLY *is standing alone in one part of the playground. Groups of boys are standing around talking, playing about etc. One such group includes* MACDOWALL *who sees Billy across the playground.*

MACDOWALL: What's up Casper, don't you like company. They say your mother does. I hear you've got more uncles than any kid in this city.

BILLY: Shut your mouth. Shut it can't you?

MACDOWALL: Come and make me.

BILLY: You can only pick on little kids. You daren't pick on anybody your own size.

MACDOWALL: Who daren't?

BILLY: You. You wouldn't say what you've just said to our Jud.

MACDOWALL: I'm not frightened of him. He's nothing your Jud. He wouldn't stick up for you anyway. He isn't even your brother.

BILLY: What is he then, my sister?

MACDOWALL: He's not your right brother, my mother says.

They don't call him Casper for a start.

BILLY: Course he's my brother. We live in the same house don't we?

MACDOWALL: You're nothing like brothers.

BILLY: I'm tellin' him! I'm tellin' him what you say Macdowall.

BILLY rushes at him but MACDOWALL *merely pushes him away without difficulty.*

MACDOWALL: Get away you squirt, before I spit on you and drown you.

BILLY rushes at him again and they begin to fight. All the other groups of boys circle round them shouting. Before long MR FARTHING *enters and pushes his way through to the centre of the group. They stop fighting and the crowd settle down a little.*

MR FARTHING: I'm giving you lot ten seconds to get back to the yard. If I see one face after that time, I'll give its owner the biggest beating he's ever had. (*They go off, some a little slower than others.*) Now then, what's going off? Well . . . Casper?

BILLY: It was his fault.

MACDOWALL: It was him.

MR FARTHING: All right. It's the same old story—nobody's fault. I ought to send both of you to Mr Gryce. Look at the mess you've made. (BILLY *is wiping his eyes.*) And stop blubbering Casper, you're not dead yet.

MACDOWALL: He will be when I get hold of him.

MR FARTHING (*he goes up to Macdowall*): You're a brave boy aren't you Macdowall. If you're so keen on fighting why don't you pick on somebody your own size? (MR FARTHING *starts poking him.*) Because you're scared aren't you Macdowall? You're nothing but a bully, the classic example of a bully. What would you say if I pinned you to the floor and smacked you across the face? (*He begins prodding him harder.*)

MACDOWALL: I'll tell my dad.

MR FARTHING: Of course you will lad. Boys like you always tell their dads. And then do you know what I'll do Macdowall? I'll tell mine. (*He begins to shout.*) So what's going to happen to your dad then. Eh? And what's going to happen to you? Eh? Eh Macdowall? (*He let's Macdowall go.*) Right, get back into school, get cleaned up and get to your lesson. And let that be the last time that you even think about bullying. UNDERSTAND?

MACDOWALL: Yes sir. (*He goes.*)

MR FARTHING: Now then, Casper, what's it all about?

BILLY: I can't tell you right sir.

MR FARTHING: Why can't you? (*Pause*)

BILLY: Well . . . he started calling me names and saying things about my mother and our Jud and everybody was laughing and . . . (*He starts crying.*)

MR FARTHING: All right lad, calm down. It's finished with now. I don't know, you always seem to be in trouble. I wonder why. Why do you think it is?

BILLY: Because everybody picks on me, that's why.

MR FARTHING: Perhaps it's because you're a bad lad.

BILLY: Perhaps I am sometimes. But I'm no worse than lots of kids and they seem to get away with it.

MR FARTHING: You think you're just unlucky then?

BILLY: I don't know sir. I seem to get into bother for daft things. Like this morning in the hall. I wasn't doing anything. I just dozed off. I'd been up since seven, then I had to run round with the papers, then run home to have a look at the hawk, then run to school. You'd have been tired if you'd done that sir.

MR FARTHING: I'd have been exhausted.

BILLY: It's nothing to get the stick for though sir. You can't tell Gryce—Mr Gryce—though, or he'd kill you. And this morning in English when I wasn't listening. It wasn't that I wasn't bothered, it was my backside, it was killing me. You can't concentrate when your backside's stinging like mad.

MR FARTHING: No, I don't suppose you can.

BILLY: Teachers never think it might be their fault either.

MR FARTHING: No, I don't think many do lad.

BILLY: Like when you get thumped for not listening when it's dead boring. You can't help not listening when it's not interesting. Can you sir?

MR FARTHING: No you can't Casper. (*Pause.* BILLY *looks down and starts playing with his hands.*) How are things at home these days?

BILLY: All right, same as usual I suppose.

MR FARTHING: What about the Police? Been in any trouble lately?

BILLY: No sir.

MR FARTHING: Reformed or not been caught.

BILLY: Reformed sir. There's always somebody after me though. If anything goes wrong on the estate, police always come to our house, even though I've done nothing for ages now.

MR FARTHING: Never mind lad, it'll be all right.

BILLY: Yes it will that.

MR FARTHING: Just think, you'll be leaving school in a few weeks, starting your first job, meeting fresh people. That's something to look forward to isn't it? (BILLY *hunches his shoulders and doesn't answer.*) Have you got a job yet?

BILLY: No sir. I've to see the Youth Employment bloke this afternoon.

MR FARTHING: What kind of job are you after?

BILLY: I shan't have much choice, shall I? I shall have to take what they've got.

MR FARTHING: I thought you'd have been looking forward to leaving.

BILLY: I'm not bothered.

MR FARTHING: I thought you didn't like school.

BILLY: I don't but that don't mean that I'll like work does it? Still, I'll get paid for not liking it, that's one thing.

MR FARTHING: Yes. Well I'll have to blow the whistle. (BILLY *begins to leave.*) Oh Casper.

BILLY: What sir?

MR FARTHING: This hawk of yours. I'd like to see it sometime.

BILLY: Yes sir.

MR FARTHING: When do you fly it?

BILLY: Dinner times. Get's dark too early at nights.

MR FARTHING: Do you fly it at home?

BILLY: Yes.

MR FARTHING: Woods Avenue, isn't it?

BILLY: Yes sir, 124.

MR FARTHING: Good, I'll be down then sometime if that's O.K.

BILLY: 'Course. (*Whistle blows.*)

END OF ACT I

ACT TWO

Scene 14: THE P. E. CHANGING ROOM

Before the scene begins properly the P.E. CLASS *enter walking casually. They are talking among themselves in the normal way.* MARTIN *and* ALLEN *are standing at the front of the group talking.*

MARTIN: I hate P.E. with him. It's always football. This weather as well.

ALLEN: We haven't been in the Gym for years now.

MARTIN: Other classes do basketball sometimes.

ALLEN: Where is he anyway? Is he here today?

MARTIN: Oh he'll be here all right. He wouldn't miss double football for anything.

SUGDEN *runs into the changing room and twice round it.*

SUGDEN: Right lads. No time for shirking. Let's have you changed. Changed and out. You should be pushing at the door fully kitted up shouting, 'Let's get out sir, to the field, to the field'.

(BILLY *enters.*)

Skyving again Casper?

BILLY: No Sir, Mr Farthing wanted me—he's been talking to me.

SUGDEN: I bet that was stimulating for him, wasn't it?

BILLY: What does that mean sir?

SUGDEN: The conversation, lad, what do you think it means?

BILLY: No sir, that word, stimu . . . stimu . . . la . . . tin.

SUGDEN: Stimulating you fool—S—T—I—M—U—L—A—T —I—N—G stimulating.

BILLY: Yes sir.

SUGDEN: Well get changed lad—You're two weeks late already. (*Looks at watch.*) Some of us want a game even if you don't.

BILLY: I've no kit sir. (*Pause*)

SUGDEN: Casper. You make me SICK. Every lesson it's the same old story. 'Please Sir, I've got no kit.' Every lesson for five years! And in all that time you've made no attempt whatsoever to get any kit. You've skyved and scrounged and borrowed and . . . Why is it that everyone else can get some, but you can't.

BILLY: I don't know sir. My mother won't buy me any. She says it's a waste of money, especially now that I'm leaving.

SUGDEN: You've not been leaving for five years have you?

BILLY: No sir.

SUGDEN: You could have bought some out of your spending money, couldn't you?

BILLY: I don't like football sir.

SUGDEN: What's that got to do with it?

BILLY: I don't know sir. Anyway I don't get enough.

SUGDEN: You should get a job then, I don't . . .

BILLY: I've got one sir.

SUGDEN: Well then, you get paid don't you?

BILLY: Yes sir, but I've to give it to my mam. I'm still paying her for my fines, like instalments every week.

SUGDEN *bounces the ball on his head.*

SUGDEN: Well you should keep out of trouble then lad, and then . . .

BILLY: I've not been in trouble sir, not . . .

SUGDEN: Shut up lad! Shut up, before you drive me crackers. (*He hits him with the ball twice. He goes into his room and brings out a giant pair of drawers.*) Here Casper, get them on. (*He throws them at Billy.*)

BILLY: They'll not fit me sir. (*The class laugh.*)

SUGDEN: What are you talking about lad. You can get them on, can't you?

BILLY: Yes sir.

SUGDEN: Well they fit you then. Now get changed. Quick.

BILLY *gets changed into the shorts.*

SUGDEN: You, Palmer come here lad.

PALMER: What sir?

SUGDEN: Ten press-ups. Come on. With me.

PALMER: I can't do press-ups sir.

SUGDEN: No I don't suppose you can. Get down.

They both begin doing press-ups as everyone continues

getting changed. After three, SUGDEN *begins to tire and he only just manages four. The boy is still going strong.* SUGDEN *stops.*

SUGDEN (*panting*): Yes, well . . . er . . . that's enough lad. You don't want to injure yourself.

The class laugh out loud at BILLY *who has now got his 'shorts' on. The tops of them are up to his chest, and the bottoms below his knees.*

SUGDEN: Roll them down and don't be so foolish. You're too daft to laugh at Casper. Right get lined up. Let's get two sides picked. Tibbut, come out here and be the other captain. (BILLY *jumps to keep warm.*) Stop prancing Casper, are you mad?

BILLY: I'm frozen sir. I'm just jumping to keep warm.

SUGDEN: Well don't lad. I'll have first pick Tibbut.

TIBBUT: That's not right sir.

SUGDEN: Why isn't it right?

TIBBUT: 'Cos you'll get all the best players.

SUGDEN: Rubbish lad.

TIBBUT: 'Course you will sir, it's not fair.

SUGDEN: Tibbut. Do you want to play football or do you want to get dressed and do maths?

TIBBUT: Football sir.

SUGDEN: Right then, stop moaning and start picking. I'll have . . .

(SUGDEN *and* TIBBUT *use the real names of the characters or make them up and two sides are picked.* SUGDEN *takes a coin from his tracksuit bottoms and tosses it.*)

SUGDEN: Call Tibbut.

TIBBUT: Tails.

SUGDEN: It's heads. We'll play downhill. Are we all ready to go? Casper. What position are you?

BILLY: Don't know sir—I've not decided yet.

SUGDEN: Goal, Casper. You'll go in goal, you're no good out.

BILLY: Oh sir, I can't goal, I'm no good.

SUGDEN: Now's your chance to learn then isn't it?

BILLY: I'm fed up of going in goal. I go in every week. Don't blame me when I let 'em all through.

SUGDEN: Of course I'll blame you lad! Who do you expect me to blame?

TIBBUT: Who are you today sir, Liverpool?

SUGDEN: Rubbish lad, don't you know your club colours yet?

TIBBUT: Liverpool are red aren't they sir?

SUGDEN: Yes, but they're all red, shirts, shorts and stockings. These are Manchester United's colours.

TIBBUT: 'Course they are sir, I forgot. What position are you playing?

SUGDEN *turns round to reveal a No. 9 on his back.*

SUGDEN: Bobby Charlton.

TIBBUT: Bobby Charlton? I thought you were usually Dennis Law when you were Manchester United?

SUGDEN: It's too cold to play as a striker today. I'm scheming this morning, all over the field, just like Charlton used to do.

TIBBUT: Law played all over sir. He wasn't just a striker.

SUGDEN: He didn't link like Charlton.

TIBBUT: Better player though sir.

SUGDEN: Are you trying to tell me about football Tibbut?

TIBBUT: No sir.

SUGDEN: Well shut up then. Anyway Law's in the wash this week.

MARTIN: Let's go sir. It's getting cold standing here.

SUGDEN (*points to Martin*): Watch it lad! Right get lined up.

(SUGDEN *now imitates a television football commentator.*)
. . . And both teams are now lined up ready to come out for this vital fifth round cup tie, Manchester United versus . . . Who are we playing Tibbut?

TIBBUT *looks round at the team lined up behind him dressed in multi-coloured kit.*

TIBBUT: Er . . . We'll be Liverpool sir.

SUGDEN: You can't be Liverpool lad, there'll be a clash of colours.

He looks again.

TIBBUT: Er . . . we'll be Spurs then sir, then there'll be no clash of colours.

SUGDEN: . . . And it's Manchester United versus Spurs in this vital fifth round cup tie. And the teams are ready. And I think that they're about to come out. Yes here they come. The teams are coming out. I can see them. They're here. They're here. Just listen to that roar.

Scene 15: BILLY'S HOUSE

BILLY *comes into the house and has a drink of milk from the bottle on the table. He sees two 10p pieces and a betting slip that Jud has left for him to take to the bookmakers. He reads it slowly.*

BILLY: 20p Double 'Crackpot', 'Tell him he's dead'. Jud. Bloody hell. (*He picks up the money.*)
Heads I take it. Tails I don't. (*Tosses coin.*) Heads . . . best out of 3. (*Tosses again.*) Tails. (*He grins slightly to himself. Tosses again.*) Heads . . . shit.
He folds the slip of paper and puts it and the money in his pocket. He goes to the hut to see Kes before going to the bookmakers.

Scene 16: KES'S HUT

BILLY *is about to go after checking that Kes is all right when* MR FARTHING *approaches*

MR FARTHING: Casper.

BILLY (*quietly*): Bloody hell fire.

MR FARTHING: Can I have a look?

BILLY: 'Course. Not too close though sir, he's nervous today. Don't know why.

MR FARTHING: Beautiful isn't it? Do you know, this is the first time I've really been close to a hawk. (*He touches the door of the hut but snatches his hand back.*) Goodness, not very friendly. Seems all right with you though.

BILLY: Only because I'm not bothered though.

MR FARTHING: How do you mean?

BILLY: Well when he used to peck me—when I first had him—I kept my finger there as though it didn't hurt. So after a bit he packed it in.

MR FARTHING: I'd never have thought of that. (*Pause*) You think a lot about that bird don't you?

BILLY: 'Course I do. Wouldn't you if it was yours? I had a little

fox cub once, reared it and let it go. It was a little blinder.
I've kept loads of birds as well.

MR FARTHING: Which was your favourite?

BILLY *stares at him, surprised that he has asked such a
question.*

BILLY: You what sir?

MR FARTHING: You mean the hawk?

BILLY: The others weren't in the same class.

MR FARTHING: What's so special about this one then?(*Pause*)

BILLY: I don't know right. It just is that's all.

MR FARTHING: What I like about it is its shape. It's so
beautifully proportioned. The neat head. The way the wings
fold over the back. And that down on its thighs—just like
plus-fours.

BILLY: It's when it's flying though, sir, that's when it's got it
over other birds; that's when it's at its best. (*Pause*) Do you
know sir, I feel as though he's doing me a favour just letting
me stand here and look at him.

MR FARTHING: It's proud of itself. It demands respect from
you.

BILLY: That's why it makes me mad when I take him out and
somebody says, 'Look at Billy Casper with his pet hawk'. I
could shout at them. It's not a pet, sir, hawks are not pets.
It's not tame, it's trained that's all. It's fierce and it's wild
and it's not bothered about anybody. Not even me right.
And that's why it's great.

MR FARTHING: A lot of people wouldn't understand that
though. They like pets they can make friends with; make a
fuss of, cuddle a bit, boss a bit. Don't you agree?

BILLY: Yes, I suppose so, but I'm not bothered about that
though. I'd sooner have him just to look at him and fly him.
That's enough for me. They can keep their rabbits and their
budgies, they're rubbish compared with him.

MR FARTHING: Yes, I think you're right. It's difficult when you
try to think why though. It's not its size is it? It doesn't look
particularly fearsome either; in fact it sometimes looks
positively babyish.

BILLY: Yes sir.

MR FARTHING: I think it's a kind of pride, a kind of
independence. It seems to have a satisfaction with its own

beauty. It seems to look you in the eye and say, "who are you anyway?" (*Pause. Then he looks at his watch*) Good lord! Look at the time. We'd better be off. I'll give you a lift if you like.

BILLY: It's all right sir.

MR FARTHING: What's a matter, would your reputation suffer if you were seen travelling with a teacher?

BILLY: It's not that. I've got one or two things to do first.

MR FARTHING: Right. I'll be off then. Don't be late. And thanks a lot, I enjoyed that.

They go off in different directions.

Scene 17: BOOKMAKER'S SHOP

People are sitting around on chairs, some looking at newspapers, some waiting for the next race to begin. MRS ROSE *is taking bets behind the counter.* BILLY *enters.*

MRS ROSE: Can I help you, lad?

BILLY: No it's all right.

He looks round, sees a space on a bench next to one of the men reading a newspaper and sits down. After a short time BILLY *speaks.*

BILLY (*holding out Jud's betting slip*): I say mister, what price are these two?

MAN: What are they? (*He takes the betting slip.*) 'Crackpot' . . . 100-6, And 'Tell him he's dead', that's . . . where is it? I've just been looking at that myself. 'Tell . . . him . . . he's . . . dead', here it is . . . 4-1 favourite.

(*Gives the slip back to Billy.*) 100-6 and 4-1.

Pause. BILLY *looks down at the slip.*

BILLY: Have they got a chance?

MAN: Now then lad, how do I know?

BILLY: Would you back them? (THE MAN *consults the newspaper again.*)

MAN: 'Tel him he's dead' has got a good chance. It's top weight. It's the best horse in the race. It must be or it wouldn't be the top weight would it? I don't fancy the other though. No form. Not even a jockey on it in here. It'll have a lad on it you can bet. No I wouldn't bother with that one.

BILLY: You don't think they'll win then?

MAN: How've you got them—doubled?

BILLY: They're not mine, they're our Jud's.

MAN: He'll be all right if they do—I can't see it myself though.

BILLY *stands up, walks round a little thinking what to do. He finally screws up the betting slip, drops it in the bin and goes out.*

BILLY: Thanks mister.

Scene 18: THE BUTCHER'S SHOP

MR BEAL, *the Butcher, is cutting meat on the counter as* BILLY *enters eating chips.*

BILLY: Quarter of beef.

MR BEAL: My, them smell good.

BILLY: Do you want one?

MR BEAL (*taking a few*): Lovely. Got them from Mrs Hartley's have you?

BILLY: That's right.

MR BEAL: Makes good chips does Mrs Hartley. (BILLY *continues eating the chips as* MR BEAL *begins to get the meat for him.*) Quarter of beef you say?

BILLY: Yes.

MR BEAL: You've still got that bird then?

BILLY: Yes.

MR BEAL (*wraps the meat up*): Here, you can have that.

BILLY: For nothing?

MR BEAL: They're only scraps.

BILLY: Thanks. Do you want another chip?
MR BEAL: No, I'll be going for my dinner in a bit.
BILLY: Cheerio, then.
MR BEAL: So long.

Scene 19: A SCHOOL CORRIDOR

Two boys, DELAMORE *and* GIBBS *are standing discussing what lessons they are supposed to go to next.* JUD *enters the school, very annoyed.*

JUD: Have you seen our Billy?
DELAMORE: Billy who?
JUD: Casper.
DELAMORE: No, not lately.
GIBBS: I haven't either.
JUD: Do you know him?
DELAMORE: 'Course I know him.
GIBBS: 'Course we know him.
JUD: Do you think you will see him?
DELAMORE: Don't know, might do might not.
GIBBS: Just depends.
JUD: If you do, tell him you've seen me.
DELAMORE: What do you want him for anyway?
JUD: He should have put a bet on for me but he didn't. He kept the money.
    JUD *goes off.* DELÀMORE *and* GIBBS *are about to do the same when they see* BILLY.
GIBBS: Hey, Casper, have you seen your Jud yet?
BILLY: No—why?
DELAMORE: He wants you, he's in school somewhere.
BILLY: What for?
GIBBS: He's been hanging around a bit now. He's just been here looking for you.
BILLY: What for though?

DELAMORE: I don't know. Something about a bet.

BILLY: Christ. How long ago?

GIBBS: 'Couple of minutes. We were just coming out of French. He was waiting outside. He must have thought that you were in our class.

DELAMORE: I reckon he's going to thump you one. I should watch out.

GIBBS: He looked right mad.

DELAMORE *and* GIBBS *go off as* PALMER *and* ROGERS *enter*.

BILLY: I say, have you seen our Jud?

PALMER: Where've you been? They've been looking all over for you.

BILLY: Who has?

PALMER: Gryce pudding and everybody.

BILLY: What for—I haven't done anything.

ROGERS: Youth Employment. You should have gone for your interview last lesson.

BILLY: Have you seen our Jud though?

ROGERS: Earlier on—over near the boiler room—why?

BILLY: Did he say anything?

PALMER: He just asked where you were that's all. What you hiding from him for?

BILLY: Have you seen him since?

ROGERS: What's the matter—is he after you for something?

GRYCE *enters behind Billy. The other two see him and immediately go.* GRYCE *hits Billy twice.*

GRYCE (*shouting*): And where do you think you've been lad?

BILLY: Nowhere sir.

GRYCE: Nowhere? Don't talk ridiculous lad. Who do you think you are—the invisible man?

BILLY: I felt sick sir—so I went to the lavatory.

GRYCE: And where were you—down it? I sent prefects to the toilets. They said you weren't there.

BILLY: I went outside then sir, for a breath of fresh air.

GRYCE: I'll give you fresh air.

BILLY: I've just come back in, sir.

GRYCE: And what about your interview? I've had the whole school out looking for you.

BILLY: I'm just going sir.

GRYCE: Well get off then. And God help anyone who employs you.

BILLY: Er . . . where to sir?

GRYCE: The medical room lad. If you'd stay awake in assembly you'd know where to. (BILLY *exits quickly.* GRYCE *also goes off but almost walks into a young pupil.*)

GRYCE: Get over lad. Don't you know to keep to the right hand side yet?

Scene 20: THE MEDICAL ROOM

On one side of the stage the YOUTH EMPLOYMENT OFFICER, *a* MOTHER *and her* SON *are talking although they cannot be heard because they are 'inside' the room. On the other side of the stage are three chairs.* BILLY *enters and sits on one of these. Before long he begins to fidget as he is impatient and also worried about Jud being in school. He stands up, walks round and sits down again.* ALLENDER *and his* MOTHER *enter and sit on the other two chairs.* BILLY *and* ALLENDER *nod to each other. Pause.*

MRS ALLENDER: And don't be sat there like a dummy when you get in. Tell him you're after a good job. An office job. Something like that.

ALLENDER: Who's after an office job?

MRS ALLENDER: Well what are you after then? A job on the bins?

ALLENDER: I wish you'd shut up.

MRS ALLENDER: Straighten your tie.

ALLENDER: I wish you'd stop nagging.

MRS ALLENDER: Somebody's got to nag.

ALLENDER: I wish you'd go home.

BILLY: Is it your mam?

The MOTHER *and* SON *'inside' the office shake hands with the Youth Employment Officer and leave. The* TWO

MOTHERS *smile at each other and pass comments on the weather.*

YOUTH EMP. OFFICER: Next. (BILLY *looks round and then goes in.*) Well come in lad if you're coming. I haven't got all day. Sit down Walker.

BILLY: I'm not Walker.

YOUTH EMP. OFFICER: Well who are you then? According to my list it should be Gerald Walker next. (*He checks his list.*) Oliver, Stenton, then Walker.

BILLY: I'm Casper.

YOUTH EMP. OFFICER: Casper? . . . Casper? Oh yes, I should have seen you earlier shouldn't I. (*He finds Billy's card.*) Casper . . . Casper. Here we are. Mmmm. Now then Casper, what kind of job have you in mind. (*Pause*) Well?

BILLY: Don't know. Haven't thought about it right.

YOUTH EMP. OFFICER: Well, you should be thinking about it. You want to start off on the right foot don't you?

BILLY: I suppose so.

YOUTH EMP. OFFICER: You haven't looked around for anything yet then?

BILLY: No, not yet.

YOUTH EMP. OFFICER: Right then. Would you like to work in an office? Or would you prefer manual work?

BILLY: What's that . . . manual work?

YOUTH EMP. OFFICER: It means working with your hands, for example, building, farming, engineering. Jobs like that, as opposed to pen-pushing jobs.

BILLY: I'd be all right working in an office, wouldn't I? I've a job to read and write.

YOUTH EMP. OFFICER: Have you thought about entering a trade as an apprentice? You know, as an electrician, or a bricklayer or something like that. Of course the money isn't too good while you're serving your apprenticeship. You may find that lads of your own age who take dead end jobs will be earning far more than you; but in those jobs there's no satisfaction or security and if you do stick it out, you'll find it well worth your while. Well what do you think about it? (*No reaction from* BILLY.) As you've already said you feel better working with your hands, perhaps this would be your best bet. Of course, it would mean attending Technical College

41

and studying for various examinations but nowadays most employers encourage their lads to take advantage of these facilities and allow them time off to attend—usually one day a week. (*He gets up from his chair, looks out of the window and continues talking.*) On the other hand, if your firm wouldn't allow you time off during the day, and you were still keen to study, then you'd have to attend classes in your own time. Some lads do it for years—two or three nights a week from leaving school until their middle twenties, when some take their Higher National or even degrees. (*He turns round.*) Had you considered continuing your education in any form after leaving school? (*No reaction from* BILLY.) I say, are you listening lad?

BILLY: Yes.

YOUTH EMP. OFFICER: You don't look as though you are to me. I haven't got all day you know, I've other lads to see before four o'clock. Now then, where were we? If nothing I've mentioned already appeals to you, and if you can stand a hard day's graft and not mind getting dirty, then there are good opportunities in mining.

BILLY: I'm not going down the pit.

YOUTH EMP. OFFICER: Conditions have improved tremendously . . .

BILLY: I wouldn't be seen dead down the pit.

YOUTH EMP. OFFICER: Well, what do you want to do then? There doesn't seem to be a job in England to suit you. (*Pause*) What about hobbies. What hobbies have you got? What about gardening, or constructing Meccano sets or anything like that? (BILLY *slowly shakes his head.*) No hobbies at all? (BILLY *stands up.*)

BILLY: Can I go now?

YOUTH EMP. OFFICER: What's the matter lad? Sit down. I haven't finished yet. (*The* YOUTH EMPLOYMENT OFFICER *takes a form and begins to fill it in.*) Well, I've interviewed some lads in my time, but I've never met one like you. Half the time you're like a cat on hot bricks—the other half you're not listening. (*He picks up a booklet.*) Here, take this home and read it. It gives you all the relevant information concerned with leaving school and starting work. Things like

sickness benefits, national insurance, pensions, etc. (BILLY *is not listening at all by this time and very anxious to get out of the room.*) At the back there's a detachable form. When you want your cards fill it in and send it to the office. The address is at the top. Have you got that? (BILLY *nods.*) Well, take it then . . . and if you have any trouble getting fixed up come in and see me. O.K.? Right Casper, that's all. Tell the next boy to come in.
BILLY *hurries out leaving the* YOUTH EMPLOYMENT OFFICER *slowly shaking his head.*

Scene 21: BILLY'S HOUSE

BILLY *is heard shouting before he enters.*

BILLY: Kes!
   He runs over to Kes's hut, but the door to it is open.
   Kes!
   He hurries into the kitchen
   Jud . . . Jud! Mother!
   He goes back towards the hut.
   Kes! Jud!
   He runs off.
   Kes! Kes!

Scene 22: THE HIGH STREET

MRS ROSE *from the bookmakers enters.* BILLY *runs up to her.*

BILLY: Hey, Mrs Rose. (*He pauses for breath.*) Have you seen our Jud?

MRS ROSE: I can see that you haven't or else you wouldn't be in one piece now.

BILLY: You've seen him then?

MRS ROSE: Seen him? He nearly ripped the place apart, that's all.

BILLY: Have you seen him since?

MRS ROSE: He called me all the names under the sun. He said I was trying to rob his eyes out. Then he threatened Tommy Leach with violence when he tried to put a word in so Tommy walked out of the shop. 'You do right', I said to Tommy. A right pantomime. I had to send for Eric Clough and Eric Street in the end to prove that you never placed that bet.

BILLY: Has he been back?

MRS ROSE: They both won, you know. 'Crackpot' got 100-8, 'Tell him he's dead' got four to one. He'd have had £13 to draw.

BILLY: Do you know where he is now?

MRS ROSE: Why didn't you put it on?

BILLY (*beginning to cry*): How do I know. I didn't know they were going to win did I?

MRS ROSE: You won't half get into trouble lad, when he gets hold of you.

BILLY *runs off*.

Scene 23: BILLY'S HOUSE

MRS CASPER *and* JUD *are casually eating tea and reading a newspaper and a magazine.*
BILLY *enters. It has been raining and he is wet.*

BILLY: Where is it? What have you done with it?

MRS CASPER: And where do you think you've been all this time? You're sodden. Get some tea. (*She goes back to her magazine.*) And shut that door Billy. There's a terrible draught behind you.

BILLY (*shouting*): I said where is it?

JUD (*shouting back at him*): What are you staring at?

MRS CASPER: What's going off. What's all this bloody shouting about?

BILLY: Ask him. He knows what it's about.

JUD (*getting up from the table*): Yes lad, and you'd have known if I'd have got hold of you earlier.

MRS CASPER: Known what? What are you both talking about. (BILLY *begins to cry.*) Now then, what's the matter with you. What have you done to him now Jud?

JUD: It's his fault. If he'd have put that bet on like he was told, there would have been none of this.

MRS CASPER: Didn't he? Well I told him before I went to work this morning.

JUD: Did he, bloody hell.

MRS CASPER: I told you not to forget Billy.

JUD: He didn't forget—he kept the money.

MRS CASPER: And what happened? Did they win?

JUD: Win? I'd have had £13 to draw if he'd kept his thieving hands to himself.

MRS CASPER: £13. Billy, you've done it once too often this time.

JUD: £13. I could have had a few days off work with that. I'd have bloody killed him if I'd have got hold of him this afternoon.

MRS CASPER: What's he crying about then?

BILLY: Because he's killed my hawk instead, that's why.

MRS CASPER: You haven't, have you Jud?

BILLY: He has. I know he has. Just because he couldn't catch me.

MRS CASPER: Have you Jud?

JUD: All right then. So I've killed it. What are you going to do about it?

BILLY: Mother! (BILLY *rushes to his mother and tries to bury his face in her but she pushes him away, embarrassed.*)

MRS CASPER: Give over then Billy. Don't be so daft.

JUD: It was its own stupid fault. I was only going to let it go but it wouldn't get out of the hut. Every time I tried to shift it, it kept lashing out at my hands with its claws. Look at them, they're scratched to ribbons.

BILLY: You bastard. You big rotten bastard.

JUD: Don't call me a bastard or you'll be the next to get it.

BILLY: You bastard.

MRS CASPER: Shut up Billy. I'm not having that language in here.

BILLY: Well do something then. Do something to him.

MRS CASPER: Where is it Jud. What have you done with it?

JUD (*turning away from the table*): It's in the bin.

BILLY *runs out to two dustbins near Kes's hut. He pushes the lid off the first but there is nothing there. He does the same to the second, and among the rubbish finds Kes, dead. He looks down on it for a few seconds, leaves it there and returns to the house.* MRS CASPER *and* JUD *have continued with their tea.*

BILLY: Have you seen what he's done mam? Have you seen it?

MRS CASPER: I know love. It's a shame. But it can't be helped.

BILLY: Come and look at it though. Look what he's done.

MRS CASPER: It were a rotten trick Jud.

JUD: It were a rotten trick what he did wasn't it?

MRS CASPER: I know but you know how much he thought of that bird.

JUD: He didn't think half as much of it as I did that 13 quid.

MRS CASPER: I know, but it was a rotten trick all the same.

BILLY: It's not fair on him mam. It's not fair on him.

MRS CASPER: I know it's not but it's done now so there's nothing we can do about it is there?

BILLY: What about him. What are you going to do to him? I want you to do something to him.

MRS CASPER: What can I do? Don't be silly.

BILLY: Hit him. Give him some fist.

JUD: I'd like to see her.

MRS CASPER: Talk sense, Billy, how can I hit him?

BILLY: You never do anything to him. He gets away with everything.

MRS CASPER: O shut up now then. You've cried long enough about it.

BILLY: You're not bothered about anything you.

MRS CASPER: Of course I'm bothered. But it's only a bird. You can get another can't you? (BILLY *lunges at Jud and starts thumping him.* JUD *stands up and starts hitting him back.*) What are you doing? Billy stop it, stop it! Jud leave him alone! Stop it both of you!

She tries to come between them. BILLY *swings his fist at her. They back away and he runs out of the house.*

MRS CASPER: Billy, come back here. Come back here you young bugger.

BILLY: You'll not catch me; you'll never catch me.

Lights fade down. BILLY *walks on. He takes Kes from inside his jacket, kneels down and digs a hole with his hands. He places Kes in the hole and covers it with the soil. Fade to blackout.*

END

Production Notes

The original production of *Kes* was produced at Colley School, Sheffield with a cast of thirty males and seventeen females.

The nature of the play is intentionally episodic and the large number of scenes mean that some of them are consequently rather short. Little or no scenery as such is required as each scene can be adequately represented by the use of a few basic and obvious props. In the original production three main acting areas were used. The open area of the traditional stage was used for most of the scenes but two recurring scenes were staged in front of the proscenium. To stage right an acting area was built representing the Casper household while to stage left one was constructed to represent the backyard of the Casper house including the hut for Kes.

With 23 scenes, continuity is an important aspect of any production. The triple staging was the major factor in ensuring this as Billy Casper, seen in every scene, moved from one acting area to another. Also contributing to the continuity in the original production, however, was a series of specially produced slides projected onto a screen to one side of the stage. Used between most of the scenes these were more than just a theatrical device to fill a series of small gaps. Besides this they were able to complement the action by echoing the events or setting of the previous scene or beginning to establish some kind of mood for what was to follow.

They showed such things as the street where Billy lived, the outside of the Library that he visited, the newsagent's shop, a close-up of Billy's books and various pictures of the inside of the school.

The role of the kestrel, being central to much of the action in the story, is as important as ever but the treatment afforded it must be much different from that offered by other types of media. To present Billy Casper's kestrel either as a real bird or depicted on film or slides—all within the realms of possibility—is going to add little to a production. The strength of the kestrel lies in its influence on Billy Casper and the attitude of the boy to the bird. Consequently, rather than the process of capture and training, it is Billy Casper's attitude and respect towards the bird that a production should concentrate on establishing. It is perhaps significant that one of the most influential characters in twentieth-century drama in Samuel Beckett's *Waiting for Godot* makes no appearance at all.

The contemporary nature of the subject matter of *Kes* means that the play lends itself a great deal to improvisation either as preparation for a production or as a group activity with no end except participation. There are many characters in the play whose attitudes are worth considering. Improvisation can often lead not only to the recognition of a particular attitude but also to discovery and discussion concerning how that particular attitude may have arisen in the first place.

In preparation for the original production greater understanding of the various attitudes was gained by occasionally exchanging characters. Much time was spent on allowing the characters to tell Billy Casper what they thought of him and why, and vice versa. More importantly, perhaps, was that on some occasions Billy Casper exchanged roles with Sugden, or Gryce or even Jud. Interaction of characters in this way led not only to a more worthwhile understanding of the story but, far more importantly as far as *Kes* is concerned, to a deeper understanding of the characters involved and the attitudes that they hold.